DRAWING IS EASY

DRAWING IS EASY

A STEP-BY-STEP GUIDE

SUSIE HODGE

ARCTURUS

ARCTURUS

This edition published in 2018 by Arcturus Publishing Limited
26/27 Bickels Yard, 151–153 Bermondsey Street,
London SE1 3HA

ISBN: 978-1-78428-578-4
AD005629UK

Printed in China

Contents

Introduction

'Couldn't draw a straight line to save my life.'

How often have you heard (or maybe said) that? People tend to say it when they lack confidence in their drawing abilities. They may have decided that as there was 'no artistic streak in the family' that it's not really worth trying. Or they may be too self-conscious to try. Or they may not know how to begin.

Just like every other activity, your drawing skills will be improved if you learn basic principles and get some practice. You can learn to draw, and without years of studying. The key to learning about drawing, just like learning to write, is some sound instruction to give you ways of approaching drawing, and then working at it until you attain the appropriate skills. It's challenging, yes, but if you can write your name you can draw. And just as your handwriting is unique to you, so your personal style of drawing will be unique. With time and some effort, you can become extremely accomplished.

Interestingly, few young children think they can't draw. Until about the age of 11, most of us do so with confidence and conviction. From a person to a fire engine, a tree to a city, nothing is too difficult; take a wax crayon or pencil and paper, and all is possible. Then everything changes after the first decade of life when we develop critical skills and become acutely aware of what we can and can't do in art. Suddenly, we become embarrassed because our artwork seems childish; we become self-conscious and dissatisfied with what we can manage – it doesn't look on paper as it does in our heads or in the world around us – and so many of us go through the rest of our school years convinced that we can't draw. Many of us stop drawing altogether.

But, logically, drawing is simply making marks, which most of us can do. I know what you're thinking: 'Oh yes, and singing is just making sounds.' But while we can't all be amazing singers, or artists at the level of perhaps Leonardo da Vinci (1452–1519), Michelangelo (1475–1564) or Vincent van Gogh (1853–90), we can all draw, and we can all improve how we do it.

This book is here to help build your confidence in your drawing abilities by showing how you can improve. Whether you're a beginner, a bit rusty, quite a good draughtsperson or a budding expert, there are tips and advice, suggestions and solutions, and several step-by-step projects to help you create drawings from the first marks to finished, fully resolved images. The book guides you through all sorts of issues, focusing on broad techniques and specific drawings, encouraging you and suggesting ways you can correct mistakes. It includes ideas from traditional methods of learning to draw as well as new ideas that you might not have encountered but that can be extremely helpful.

All drawing is a case of studied observation, rather than just assuming you know what your world looks like. Look carefully at spaces, proportions, textures and where the light falls, and judge how you might represent them all on paper.. This takes patience, practice, a recognition of any mistakes and a little knowledge. Trial and error are important too, of course, but rather than spending a lot of time making those errors hopefully this book will help you to spot potential pitfalls and common mistakes before you make them – or, if not, it will at least help you to correct them with growing confidence.

Drawing like any skill improves with practice. So please don't give up if you make errors. Mistakes are imperative really; they are an important way in which we all learn and so improve. Some art teachers insist that all mistakes should be left where they are; you just draw over them. The theory is you don't make the same error again. Other ways of recognizing your mistakes are to hold your drawing up in front of a mirror or to take a photograph of it, or to put it aside for at least twenty-four hours. With any of these methods, you will be looking at your work with fresh, more objective eyes. Yet another way of improving is to ask others what they think. Not everyone will tell you the truth, of course, and never let another person's opinions about your drawings get you down, but it's worth asking and then trying to look at your work from a different viewpoint.

Being a good drawer is not a matter of being able to draw a straight line without a ruler. So take heart and don't be put off by imperfections!

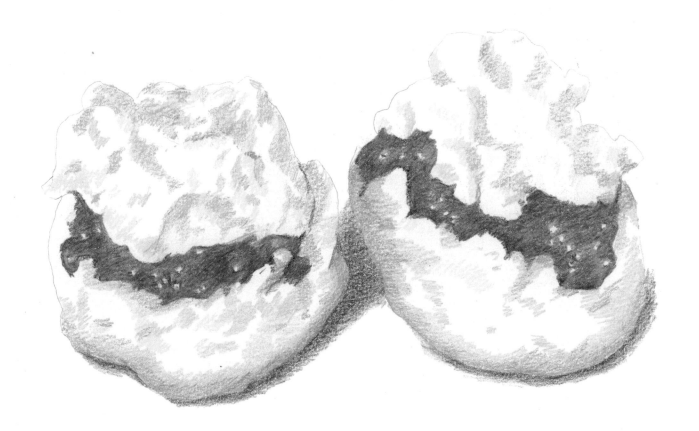

Materials

Drawing with a pencil on paper is one of the most inexpensive forms of art, but there are plenty of other wonderful materials you can use.

PENCILS

Being one of the most common implements used to make marks, there are many different kinds, but the most popular are lead pencils, which were first made in the 16th century after graphite was discovered in Cumbria, England. The first people to put sticks of graphite into wooden holders were Italian, but the French inventor Nicolas-Jacques Conté (1755–1805) was the first to create different hardnesses of graphite. Conté mixed powdered graphite with clay and formed the mixture into sticks that were then fired in a kiln. By varying the amount of graphite and clay, he modified its hardness or softness.

The letter on the side of a pencil tells you its hardness. H stands for hard and B for black (or soft), so an HB is a medium pencil, while a 2H is fairly hard and a 4B is soft. The higher the number, the harder or softer the pencil becomes (6B, for example, is softer than 2B). Tonal work can be more effective with softer pencils, as the softness allows you to blend smoothly and erase without leaving indents if you make a mistake. Mechanical pencils are good for precision work.

GRAPHITE STICKS

Being solid graphite, usually without a wooden or plastic pencil casing, graphite sticks will make your fingers black, yet they are great for blending, using either the tip or the sides of the stick. Some have a lacquer coating or paper covering to protect your fingers, and some are water-soluble and can be blended with water for interesting effects.

CHALK

A hard stick of white chalk can be used to make details on coloured paper, or a soft pastel one can be blended more easily. Chalk was often used by Renaissance artists on coloured paper, usually charcoal or sanguine-coloured chalks.

CHARCOAL AND CHARCOAL PENCILS

Among the earliest drawing implements used by humans were sticks of charred wood, usually willow or vine, available in different thicknesses. Thin sticks work well for creating details, while block charcoal is good for large areas. Compressed charcoal produces dark, black marks, which can be difficult to smudge or blend. Charcoal pencils come in a wooden casing, so are less messy. They are often quite hard and can give a sharper line than other types of charcoal. Although not easy to erase, they can be effective for creating textured effects.

CONTÉ CRAYONS, STICKS AND PENCILS

These are natural pigments bound with gum arabic. The most popular colours are earth tones – white, black, greys, browns and rusts, such as sanguine and sepia – but other colours are available too. Contés are effective for crisp, decisive lines and for large areas of tone. They can be smudged smoothly, but are not easily erased.

PASTEL PENCILS

Such tools are harder than soft pastels and look like coloured pencils, although they are much chalkier. They are good for detailed line work as well as shading as they are non-waxy and can be blended well. They come in many colours.

COLOURED PENCILS

Many different colours and forms, such as standard, water-soluble and thick/thin-leaded, are available, and they vary in quality and softness. Some coloured pencils have a heavy wax content and deep pigments, some have thin leads, which make defined lines, while others are clay-based and can be blended easily. Layering colours produces different shades,

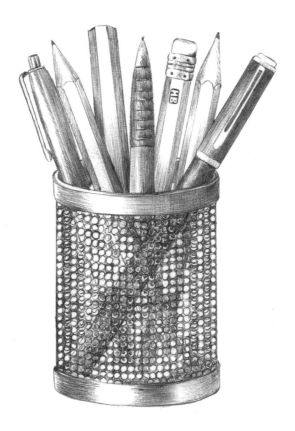

and interesting results can be achieved by using groups of colours in different sequences.

PENS
Technical pens are convenient, but the marks that can be made with them are fairly rigid. Dip pens are pen-holders with interchangeable, flexible metal nibs. Pointed nibs are best for detail, while chiselled, or calligraphy, nibs can create an effective range of textures. Fountain or cartridge pens, rollerball, ballpoint, fine-liners and specialist art pens come with a wide range of nibs and can be used for quick sketches and more detailed drawings. Ballpoint pens can be used for sketching and more detailed drawing as the depth of darkness can be varied.

INKS
Indian ink – which actually originated in China – is black, waterproof and dries fast. Other waterproof inks are available in various colours. Water-soluble ink can be diluted with water and blended to create different tones. Felt and fibre-tipped pens are made in both waterproof and water-soluble versions.

SHARPENERS
Craft knives and scalpels, with fixed or retractable blades, are good for sharpening pencils as they give you great control over the shape and sharpness of the tip. They are also good for trimming dirty edges from erasers. Regular pencil sharpeners are fine too, provided they have sharp blades. Soft ones need sharpening more often than hard pencils because the leads wear away at a faster rate as they are used.

ERASERS AND STUMPS
These are useful for erasing or 'lifting out' mistakes or for blending. Kneaded or kneadable erasers, also known as putty rubbers, can be squashed into small shapes for hard-to-reach places and for 'lifting out' highlights in heavy tonal areas. For blending charcoal, chalks and pastel pencils, use a paper stump called a torchon or a tortillon.

FIXATIVE

This is resin which has been dissolved in a colourless spirit solvent, and which prevents drawings made with pencil, charcoal or other soft-pigment materials from being smudged. When sprayed on to a drawing, the spirit solvent evaporates and a thin coating of resin is left behind, which binds the pigment dust to the support. Once a drawing is fixed, even an eraser can't alter it. It is possible, however, to work on top of a fixed drawing and it is sometimes helpful to fix a drawing periodically while it is in progress. Fixative is best applied using a CFC-free aerosol, following the manufacturer's instructions. Bottles with hand-operated sprays and mouth-spray diffusers are also available.

PAPER AND OTHER SUPPORTS

The surface of your paper determines the effect of the media used on it. Good-quality paper is neutralized to counteract acidity and will not become brown, yellowed or brittle. It is usually labelled 'acid-free'. Cartridge (drawing) paper can be white, cream or coloured and is available in various weights, sizes, thicknesses and qualities.

Pastel paper comes in a range of tints and has a 'tooth' or grain, which is designed to hold the tiny particles of colour. Usually, only one side of the paper is textured and this is the side most people draw on, but you can use either side. Pastel paper comes in two weights; thicker paper can take heavier layering, rubbing and reworking than lighter paper.

Watercolour paper is available in various weights and textures and can be good for drawing. Hot pressed (HP) paper has a smooth surface, suitable for detailed work. Cold pressed paper (NOT) has a 'tooth'. Try out textured, coloured or handmade papers, card and specialist papers with coatings, such as velour paper. These can all add interest and another dimension to your work.

Sketchbooks are made with paper and card of various surfaces, colours and weights. They come in many sizes and bindings and in both portrait and landscape formats. Experiment with different surfaces, textures and colours until you find what works best for you.

DRAWING BOARDS

Securing your paper or other support to a drawing board will make it easier for you to work. It might sound obvious, but make sure that the board is large enough for your paper and has a smooth surface. You can buy purpose-made drawing boards from good art shops or use a sheet of plywood or medium density fibreboard (MDF).

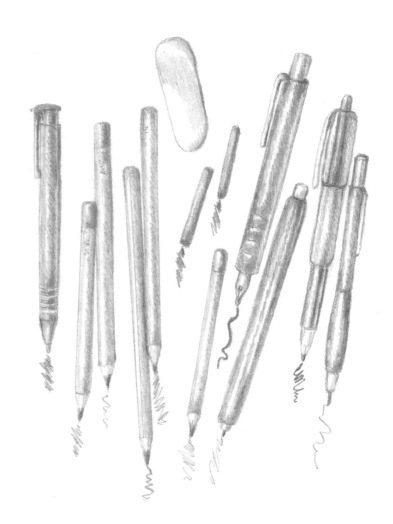

WAYS OF WORKING

When it comes to drawing, there are several things that you can do to help yourself before you even start. Remember, however, that there are really no right or wrong ways to draw.

Making mistakes

Each of us learns what is best for our individual ways of drawing, and the best way to learn is to make errors – and then fix them. Every artist does this; it's all part of the learning process and the mistakes will become fewer as you progress. So try not to be disheartened. If you study many great masters' paintings, you can often see where they have corrected their errors. However, although you might want to correct everything, don't be a perfectionist; unless you intend framing every drawing, leave in some mistakes and either draw over them or redraw the image, trying not to make the same mistake again. Many art teachers forbid the use of erasers for this reason; they insist that knowing that you can't simply erase something focuses the mind.

Think about your posture

You may prefer working at a desk, on a drawing board or at an easel. Think of your neck! Bending over flat work for long periods can put a great strain on your neck and head – and even your shoulders – so try to draw with your paper at an incline, tilted on a drawing board or easel. And remember to roll your shoulders and tilt your head this way and that every now and then to keep flexible.

Outlines

The real world does not have outlines. We draw them to show edges and we all know what these mean, but an attempt to draw realistically is ruined by heavy outlines. These flatten your drawings and will give them cartoon-like appearances. Outlines are useful for marking shapes in the initial stages of a drawing but should never be heavy.

Visualize

Before you begin a drawing, look at your paper and visualize your drawing on it, filling it. Then lightly sketch the underlying structure, making sure it is not too small or concentrated on only one side of the paper, and so on.

Shades of grey

If you are a beginner, concentrate on proportion, shape and structure. Worry about details only when you are more confident. And learn to use a wide range of tones, from black to white and every shade of grey in between. If you are using pencils, to get the greatest range of tones you may find it best to try a number of grades, perhaps 2B, 3B, 5B and even 8B.

Two common mistakes

There are two common stumbling blocks with drawing, which can affect experienced artists as well as beginners. The first is that when drawing from observation – something most of us do – we draw what we see in our heads rather than what's in front of us. So train yourself to really look and see what is in front of you. The second challenge is knowing when to stop. This can be extremely difficult for even the most experienced artists, but it's something that can be practised until it's attainable.

Light

Most how-to-draw books start with instructions on drawing outlines, which is the most usual and often an instinctive way of beginning to draw.

Although outlines don't exist in nature, they are an excellent way of showing different objects in drawings. However, this book is starting with light, because light is the way we see. Without it, we couldn't notice anything, and with it we can spot shapes and forms of objects as well as an understanding of depth and distance. By learning to consider ways in which light falls on objects, and to interpret this in your drawings, you will be able to make a flat drawing look like a three-dimensional one. So the perception and translation of light and shadow are among the most important skills in drawing and painting.

Tone and solidity

While lines show viewers the boundaries of your objects, tone represents depth, distance and form. Some drawings use strong tonal contrasts, while others include lighter or fewer suggestions of tone. Some artists adopt a method of smooth shading for tonal contrasts, and others introduce different

marks such as hatching, cross-hatching or stippling. You can use one form of shading or several in any drawing – it's entirely up to personal preference and the subject matter.

Creating a sense of solidity through shading is usually more effective if you draw from life rather than from photographs, because the human eye sees much more than what is in a photograph. This is not to say abandon photographs; they are great as resource material, but all drawings are interpretations and being able to see an entire scene, person or object, for example, gives you more scope, and drawing 'from life' will strengthen your observational and drawing skills. So when you're looking at anything, notice how highlights appear to come forward and dark areas seem to recede. If your paper or other support is white, use that as your highlight. If it is coloured, then you will need to create a brighter, lighter highlight, such as with white chalk, pastel, coloured pencil or gouache.

The following pages show you how to look for shapes and negative space, but first, if you become used to viewing the world in terms of tonal contrast and how you might portray it, you will be able to imbue your drawings with added sophistication and realism from the start. When you look at things – anything – notice where the light falls and where it doesn't, where objects cast shadows and what shapes they are. Look at trees, the sea, the sky, animals, faces, furniture, flowers, fruit – everything – and really notice where and how the light falls and how you might replicate that. Where is it brightest – or where does the brightest light fall? Where is it darkest? In this way you will develop the habit of viewing and considering the world in its three dimensions.

Value

Values are the different tonal shades between white and black. In drawings, a range of values creates the illusion of three dimensions, and so applying a broad range will help to make your drawings look lifelike. Drawing accurate values is the key to achieving a convincing three-dimensional illusion in your drawings.

Don't feel daunted. You might not replicate the exact values that you see in reality, but as long as you build up accurate value relationships, or the right strengths of tone, you will impart a sense of reality. To achieve this, you will probably need to use a range of pencils of varying hardnesses.

Shading boxes or squares

One of the most effective exercises for practising your skills in creating tonal values is shading boxes or squares. You can do it an infinite number of times to improve your skills, and your shading can be smooth and even, or through patterns and marks. Draw several strips as below of seven boxes or squares in a line next to each other. Use a ruler, but don't worry too much if they're not identical.

In the first line of seven boxes, do some smooth shading. Use a soft pencil for the first or darkest box, keep your pencil steady and don't press hard, but press firmly and layer either side to side, diagonally or in small circular movements. The next five squares or boxes need to show a graduated scale of tonal values, so the square next to the first, blackest square that you have just filled in has to be almost as dark as the first, but not quite. The adjacent square or box has to be shaded in a mid to dark tone and so on until the penultimate box next to the white square has to be extremely light, but still shaded. Leave the last box white. This is your spectrum of scales, the darkest to the lightest. You may find anything from a 3B to a 9B pencil useful for the darkest square and and HB or H for the square next to the white one at the other end.

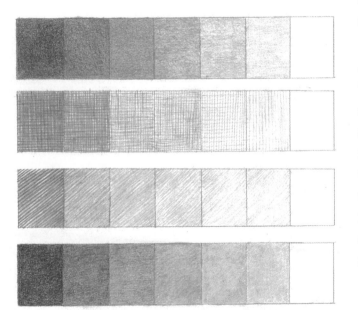

For the second set of boxes, try cross-hatching (parallel crossed lines) in a range of tones. On the row below, draw diagonal parallel lines (hatching) or stippling (dots), and in the final row introduce other patterns or coloured pencils. Here, I've used shades of grey and black coloured pencils. You can try the same exercise with charcoal and ballpoint pen.

Contrast

A strong light source helps you see the value differences more easily as it will enhance the contrast. Diffused light eliminates definite shadows and highlights, producing subtle shifts in tones. Values play a crucial role in the creation of visual illusions on flat surfaces. The best technique for seeing values and value relationships accurately is squinting – or narrowing your eyes until the image seems to go out of focus. Try it. By screening out details, you'll be able to identify the darkest and the lightest areas of anything in front of you. Notice the darkest values, and the lightest, and the shapes formed by different values.

Contrast can make your work appear more three-dimensional by creating powerful, dynamic drawings. Even low-contrast drawings, that is, with more light and middle values than dark, can still look convincingly lifelike, depending on the subject matter.

Sfumato

The most sensitive and subtle form of shading – sfumato – derives from the Italian *fumo*, meaning smoke, and describes soft or blurred tonal contrasts, most prominently used by Leonardo da Vinci in the 15th and 16th centuries. Leonardo is believed to have pioneered the technique of soft transitions from light to dark shading, writing that light and shade should blend 'without lines or borders, in the manner that gradually vanishes like smoke'. You can see the effects of this in all his paintings, such as *Mona Lisa*, in both her face and the background. Other famous artists who used sfumato include Antonio da Correggio (1489–1534), Raphael (1483–1520) and Giorgione (1478–1510).

To practise the sfumato technique, you need to work slowly and carefully, layering and keeping a smooth and steady hand. Set up a small, simple arrangement of objects and try to have only one light source, so darken your room and use light from a table lamp, torch or candle. (Make sure you can see your paper!) Draw what you see, simple outlines for now, so don't worry about accuracy – it's the shading you are focusing on; you are aiming to record the tonal contrasts of light and shade, using the soft method of sfumato. With a light and even touch, apply smooth shading, building it up with minuscule strokes and soft gradations. You are aiming for an almost blurred, hazy appearance. Keep your pencil sharp and try using different pencils for the darkest, medium and lightest tones, such as a 4B, 2B and HB.

Chiaroscuro

Another Italian term used in drawing is chiaroscuro, which means light–dark and refers to dramatically portrayed light and shade in drawings, paintings, photographs and prints. Developed during the Renaissance, its use continued into the baroque period and is still popular today. Artists including Leonardo, Caravaggio (1571–1610) and Rembrandt (1606–69) are particularly recognized for their spectacular use of the technique. Leonardo created a series of drawings to illustrate the book *De Divina Proportione* by the Franciscan friar and mathematician Luca Pacioli (1447–1517), published in 1509. The drawings are spheres that he shaded from dark to light, producing a realistic sense of solidity.

To create chiaroscuro in your drawings, you can use many different approaches including smooth areas of tone, or hatching, cross-hatching or stippling, because – unlike sfumato – chiaroscuro can show textures. The difference is the strength and dramatic contrasts between the deepest, darkest areas and the sharpest, whitest highlights.

Hard and soft

Try drawing several household items, considering them in terms of their tonal values. Squint to see where the darkest and lightest areas are. Try drawing with different materials such as ballpoint pen, coloured pencils, charcoal or chalk pastels. Each material requires slightly different techniques. For example, charcoal and chalk can be smudged to good effect, yet this would look messy with pencil and simply can't be done with ballpoint pen. Rather than simply pressing harder or softer with a pencil or pen, you can deepen tones convincingly by layering and applying slightly more or less pressure.

Draw an apple that looks 3D

Here is a circle that has been shaded to look like a 3D sphere in order to show how tonal contrasts make flat shapes look solid or three-dimensional. Try it out for yourself, then have a go at a step-by-step drawing of an apple with shading to make it look solid and realistic. You will need the following materials:

• White paper
• 2B, 4B and 6B pencils
• An eraser if necessary

1 Using a 2B pencil, lightly draw a circle. Don't worry about doing this exactly; most apples are not perfectly rounded. If you prefer, either draw around a rounded object, or else mark a square and divide it with a cross then draw curves that join in each quarter.

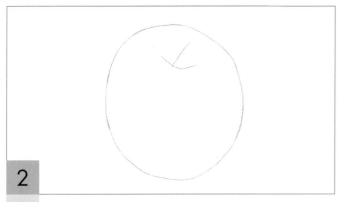

2 Mark a small curve and diagonal line to indicate the stalk source and stalk.

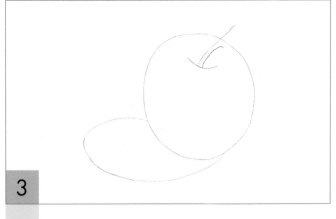

3 Draw the shape of the cast shadow, noticing how it swoops round the base of the apple.

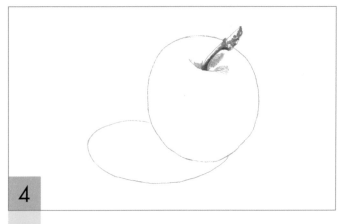

4 With the same 2B pencil, begin to add tone to the stalk, and a bit of shadow at its base. Then using the 6B pencil, add darker tones to the stalk on one side.

5

With the 4B, begin shading around the bottom of the apple and on the cast shadow, building up the shading on the side of the apple and adding tones to the cast shadow.

6

Continue shading the side of the apple; you can use smooth, straight lines or small circles, or shade in different directions, layering and leaving no white paper showing through. Add a few light lines to indicate the markings on the apple – nothing much, concentrate on the tonal values. Deepen the darkness on the stalk and work up its knobbly end, leaving some white areas as highlight.

7

Layer tone on the side of the apple and even more on the cast shadow. For the cast shadow, use the 6B with any method that suits you. Hatching or cross-hatching, or smooth shading with overlapping diagonal lines, are all effective for the apple and its shadow, although finish the apple with lines that follow its shape. Using your pencil tip, define the curve in front of the stalk.

Cutlery

Man-made objects such as cutlery are precisely shaped and smooth. They are also shiny and hard. So tonal contrasts are dramatic – strong darks and brilliant lights, because of the shine and reflections. To draw them in pencil, it's best to use a range of hardnesses. For this step-by-step drawing, I used a B, 3B and 6B.

1 Draw the outline lightly, by working out angles and proportions with your eye – forgetting that they are familiar objects and drawing only the shapes that you see.

2 Carefully mark on some of the dark tones, lightly at first and in different places. Narrow your eyes to see the darkest and lightest tones.

3 Build up the tonal marks – they are in only a few places, and where they appear they are fairly dark. Using a slightly darker, softer pencil, such as a 3B, layer over the darkest areas and build up the slight cast shadow under the items, to 'anchor' them.

Fabric

Drawing fabric convincingly is excellent in itself, simply as a method of developing drawing ability and understanding tone; the skills will help you on a broader scale, with a much wider range of subject matters. More specifically, once you can draw folds with different types and ranges of tone, you will be even better at depicting people in clothes, draped material and still lifes and at imparting a sense of movement. There are certain types of folds, and understanding them and their angles, and how to portray each with an appropriate amount of depth and volume, is a versatile skill to have. Folds do vary, but they can be categorized to make things simpler.

- **Spiral folds** occur when fabric is rolled or bunched up, usually when a body part such as an arm in a sleeve is moving.
- **Zigzag folds** are angled in different directions and often occur on shirt or blouse sleeves, or on trousers around the crotch or behind the knees.

Hanging
folds

Zigzag folds

Spiral folds

Pipe folds

- **Hanging folds** curve, swathe and sag between two points. Tablecloths, scarves and the necklines of togas often show such folds. Different amounts of fabric between the support points alter the amount of slack in the material.
- **Pipe folds** usually appear in curtains, flags, towels on pegs and other loose, hanging fabric.

Even if you can't remember the names of these types of fold, you can identify them by looking for places of tension or force created in fabric.

Depending on the thickness, softness or stiffness of the fabric, folds look different. The more the fabric is scrunched up, the closer or tighter the folds will be, while softer fabric and looser folds can be drawn with lighter tones. Stiff or crisp fabric forms angular bends in the folds. Above is a drawing of a cloth, folded randomly. Notice the difference in tones of smooth undulations and edges of folds, and really look and analyse tonal relationships. This simply means visually compare the hard and soft lines and edges, strong, dramatic contrasts of light and dark, and softer, less noticeable or more graduated changes in depth and darkness.

Step-by-step crumpled fabric drawing

This is a helpful exercise to gain insights and skills in drawing different kinds of tones, from the deepest shadows to lighter touches.

1

With a B or 2B pencil, draw the rough outline of the shape of the folded fabric. Don't grip the pencil too tightly. Draw angled lines inside the main overall shape.

2

Where necessary, soften or erase any sharp or straight lines that you have drawn.

3

Squint your eyes to see the darkest tones and their shapes and placement, then lightly begin to mark these shadowed areas in places across the image.

4

Vary the pressure of your lines as some edges can barely be seen, while others can be drawn with firm lines. Carry on building up the shadowed areas across the image. To retain balance, it's better to do this across the entire drawing rather than work in one area at a time.

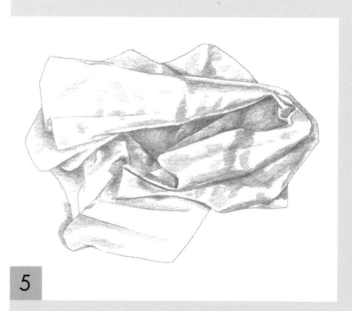

5

Add darker shading at the edges of the fabric by layering more firmly and using smooth marks. Create the darkest, deepest shadows using a softer pencil, such as a 4B or 5B. If you've accidentally smudged any marks, clean these up with a putty eraser, an ordinary eraser or a mechanical eraser.

Facial features

Before moving on to portraits (on pages 104–13), a good exercise when you're developing skills in understanding tones and how to depict them is to draw facial features. Depending on the surrounding light, most features have a balance of light and dark tones. The most effective way to create a realistic range of tones is to build them up by layering, applying light shading first and strengthening the dark areas where needed. The darkest tones are close to black, so build them up last of all, that is, after you have established the lighter and mid-tones across the image. Darkest tones are often accents: between the lips, the pupils, base of the eyelashes, nostrils, part of the eyebrows.

Have a look at facial features and consider how to make them look lifelike by using tones. For example, remember that eyeballs are spherical. The upper eyelid will probably cast shadow on the visible eyeball, so there will usually be some shading on the white of the eye, with deeper shadow above it, in the crease of the eyelid and the corners of the eyes. Depending on the angle and strength of the light, there will be highlights in the iris, possibly the pupil and also on the white of the eye. In profile, the bridge of the nose can be shown with a drawn line, but when seen from the front the nose should be indicated only by light and shading on either side, never a hard line. Under the tip there can be a firmer line and stronger tone if the light is coming from above, which is usual. On some faces, the nostrils seem to be almost black, while on other faces they can't be spotted at all. The darkest part of the mouth is usually shown as a line between the two lips. Shade lightly in the corners of the mouth and suggest the lower lip with no hard line, but a shadow underneath. The upper lip is also darker when the light shines down from above. If the mouth is open, inside will be dark; teeth will be shaded at the top, or if you can't see the teeth the inside of the mouth will appear almost as dark as the nostrils. The lips on a face in profile resemble a heart on its side, but there is no hard line around the edge; lips from the side should be suggested with tone.

Although we have looked at a few specific things in terms of tonal contrast and values in this chapter, tone is something to look for and practise drawing in everything. The ideas shown and discussed here can – and should – be translated into everything you draw.

Textures and patterns

Texture is the way an object feels, or looks as it might feel, and, depending on how you draw it, it's one of those elements that can really make your drawings come to life – or not.

A multitude of textures can be portrayed effectively in drawings. If you are a beginner, you may be surprised to know that drawing every detail of texture will make most drawings look static and unrealistic. If you're attempting to show three dimensions, put more textural marks either on areas closest to viewers, or in the darkest-toned places. Leaving the paper white will suggest highlights, and the type of texture determines the amount of light that is reflected off the surface. Hard, soft, rough or smooth, natural or man-made, all textures can be portrayed with easy marks that many of us use when doodling.

- **Hard surfaces** such as metal, glass or glazed china are highly reflective, so light hits large surface areas and bounces off, creating firm edges and strong tonal contrasts.
- **Soft surfaces** – for example, fabric or fur – absorb light, so some parts have graduated transitions between light areas and shadows.
- **Rough surfaces** – light usually falls on rough surfaces in random areas.

Little light is reflected and, what there is catches irregularly. Sharp-angled protrusions form intense variations in tone, while softer contours create smoother, less pronounced tonal contrasts.

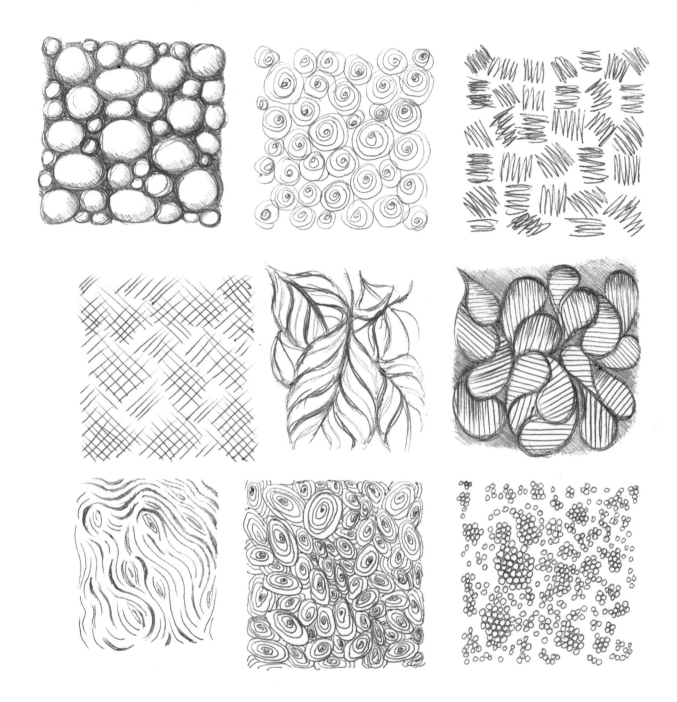

Making marks

To portray a sense of texture, don't try to draw the exact shapes and lines, but simply make different marks that give an overall sense of what the surface feels like. The skill is in using the right types of marks to convey certain textures. These marks can all be simple, such as hatching, cross-hatching, stippling, zigzags or squiggles.

An effective exercise to build your skills in rendering textures is to draw lots of different marks. Here are some to inspire you, using pencils and ballpoint pen. Notice how some have circular shapes, some have straight lines, some have broken, staccato marks and some have a mixture. They don't represent actual textures, but they could all be adapted for that.

TEXTURES AND PATTERNS

In general, as in the last chapter, while you are observing the world and forming images in your mind about how to portray tonal values, do the same for textures. Notice how many you see around you, and how they might be interpreted as marks. Make quick sketches of them. You don't have to draw the actual thing, just make marks to try to depict the surface texture. This will help you to notice textures with an artist's eye and expand your ideas about how to depict them. Another effective exercise is to think of as many words as you can to describe different textures, such as coarse, slimy, bristly, smooth, furry, matted, twisted, scratchy, wrinkled, soft, rough. Now consider how you would draw those textures in simple drawings of common things such as:

- **Tree trunks** – use rough marks on the side of the tree trunk. Don't be specific – just a rough scribble where the light does not fall. Make the branches taper away by lifting your pencil slightly off the paper.
- **Clouds** – use soft pencils and make curving shapes, surrounded by soft shading.

- **Leaves** – to create the illusion of leaves, scribble around and about to create overlapping marks and shapes. Some areas should be darker and denser than others.
- **Grass** – make roughly vertical pencil strokes, using heavier pressure at the base of the blade. Leave the paper showing to indicate where the light touches the grass and then make further dark lines for the tips of the grass. Each blade should taper at the top. Create light, wispy grass with lighter pencil strokes, and coarser grass with stronger pencil marks
- **Water** – keep your pencil sharp and leave the paper white for the large areas of highlight. The darkest tones should be sharp and wiggly, while mid-tones appear in and through the transparent liquid. Lines should be varied in lightness, and no line should be continuous. Notice shapes in small areas and use a full tonal range.

Depth, distance and pattern

When seen in close-up, many textures can be described with more detail, while from a distance the same textures and shapes become mere suggestions – masses rather than features individually described.

TEXTURES AND PATTERNS

Some drawings do not require you to show the feel of the subject except for its overall appearance, markings or patterns: for example, a garden, patterned teapot or a folded, patterned cloth. After your practice with the crumpled fabric (see page 20), this is another similar exercise, but with a pattern.

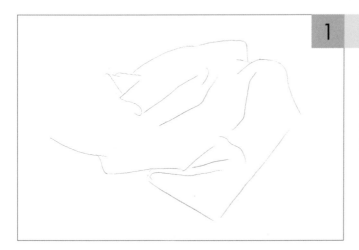

1

Take any piece of patterned fabric you have close to hand, such as a tea cloth, scarf or towel, and simply drop it down on a table top in front of you. Draw the overall shape of the cloth by looking at the shapes and angles involved, especially the negative shapes (see page 30).

2

Draw the pattern on the fabric, noticing where it curves, bends away, changes shape and disappears from view, and similarly where it reappears. Add tonal contrasts – darker under creases and folds, lighter on undulations.

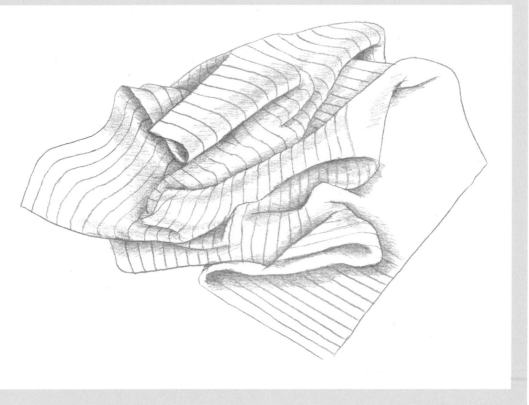

Animals

Scales, feathers and fur can all be suggested with different marks. For example, light, feathery lines at opposite angles and parallel to each other will look like feathers, especially if the marks are firm at the base, then lighter and 'feathery' at the tips. For fur, make short marks for short fur and longer ones for long fur. Observe closely the direction in which fur or feathers grow and apply marks where light does not fall, making your darkest tones out of textural rather than smooth marks. Certain breeds and species of animals have a range of characteristic markings that make patterns on their coats or skin. As long as you show tonal contrasts and some individual irregularities, these can be made to look convincing. Here are some simplified suggestions of animal markings which are worth practising. Come up with some of your own too.

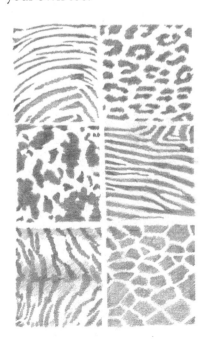

Step-by-step fir tree

This fir tree is drawn in ballpoint pen, which can be useful for fine lines, delicate marks and variegated tones.

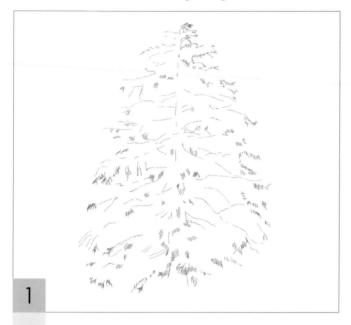

1

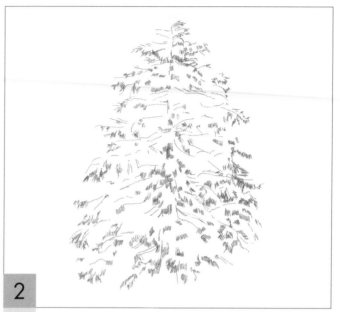

2

Start by marking parts of the trunk in broken, vertical lines in the centre of the tree, with a few indications of branches. Your lines should not be straight as tree branches grow up and out and no tree is symmetrical. Begin to suggest some of the needles using scribble-like short lines.

Build up more needles with more scribbled lines, working across the image. Again, this does not have to be precise, nor should it be symmetrical. Use a light touch.

3

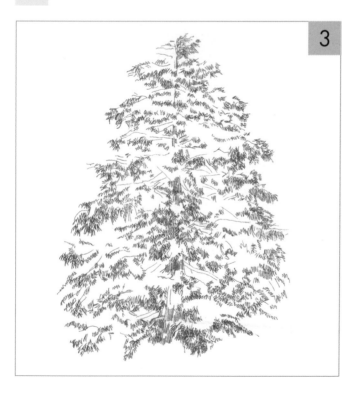

To build the illusion of depth and three dimensions, begin to emphasize deeper areas of shadow by layering or using slightly more pressure.

4

Continue working across the image, creating a rhythm. Leave areas uncovered on top of the foliage to indicate light, and make some parts seem denser underneath. Also build up a darker side on the trunk that can be seen through the branches in places.

Space and proportion

In order to draw well, you need to be objective. That is, you have to draw what you see rather than what you think you see.

You need to try to forget everything you think you 'know' about a subject in order to actually draw it as it appears. An effective way of turning off your subjective mind and drawing just what you observe in the right proportions, rather than what you think you see, is to look for the negative spaces, or shapes.

These are the spaces around and between objects rather than the objects themselves. You need to disassociate from any labelling of objects in your mind, so your brain won't tell you how to draw what it recognizes. Try not to focus solely on the object, or to label it, but see it as a simple shape. Once you have looked for the overall negative shape, search for the smaller, 'trapped' shapes and angles in between that overall outer area.

Draw those shapes as you see them – because they are not of actual things you recognize they will be easier to draw objectively. In this way, the positive shape, or the actual object, is not outlined and your mind will not have taken over; you will draw what you really see. Observing negative shapes correctly is a skill worth developing. By drawing these shapes between and around objects, the positive form of the object will be revealed. If you draw the negative shapes correctly, the positive shapes will be accurate.

Once you become skilled at this approach, you will be able to draw what you see by blending elements of positive and negative shapes. Later, you will be able to draw what you notice without worrying about it. By practising focusing your attention on negative shapes in and around all you draw, you will train yourself to capture proportions and angles more accurately.

Learning to look

It is important to really observe and closely see the things that will help you to make your drawings more realistic, including negative shapes, tonal contrasts, placement and shapes, textures and patterns. So you need to develop skills in looking and translating all this on to your paper.

The chair (left) and female figure and hands (above) are shown only by their negative spaces. Notice the proportions and irregular shapes, and try drawing other objects in the same way; it will help your observational skills.

Putting it together

If you keep the idea of negative shapes in mind, as well as comparing sizes and proportions, and then adding tone and texture, you'll find you can draw a fairly convincing cat washing itself.

1 This is a cat sitting in profile, with one paw on the ground. When drawing, look for negative shapes and also at proportions. For example, how large is the cat's head in comparison with its leg? What about in comparison with the part of the body you can see?

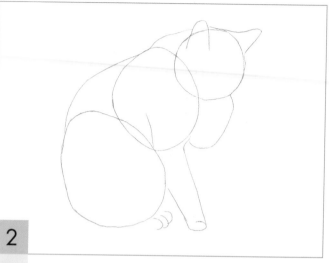

2 After breaking down the body into three, notice the triangular shape between the right foreleg and haunch, and show how the left foreleg is bent upwards – it's shorter than the length of the head. The ears are smaller again.

3 Now begin joining up the shapes of the body, still paying attention to the negative shapes around the animal. As you add parts such as the tail, the eyes and tongue, erase your original guidelines.

4 Begin to add texture and tone, using short marks here and there; build up the limbs and add whiskers. Work across the drawing, never in one place only.

5

This is the bit that takes the most time – the finishing off. Using a sharp pencil, scribble with short marks in the direction the fur grows, to convey the appearance of short cat fur, texture, tone and markings. Layer and press slightly more in areas where the light does not reach, including under the front right paw, behind the tongue, around the base and tip of the tail, behind the paw on the face and on the cat's back.

Relationships

As with the drawing of a cat washing itself, as you are drawing it is important to be aware of the whole object or objects, so you can envisage the proportions. Similarly, as you look at your paper, or whatever support you are using, imagine your finished drawing on it. This will ensure that you fill the space. It will help you to place all elements in more or less correct proportions, even if they're not completely accurate. And it will prevent you from drawing your image too far to one side, or too small or too large, for example.

To achieve accurate proportions, look at relationships of sizes and spaces between and within objects. Compare angles between objects and the shapes of shadows, for example. See if you can identify geometric shapes next to and between things, and how they compare to each other – ratios

and proportions. These can be wherever you think of them – use as many measurements or assessments as you feel you need. In this still life, I've shown, in orange felt tip, some of the relationships, shapes and angles I compared to make the grouping look right.

5

When you are comfortable with all the spaces and proportions on your face, build up tones and flowing lines for hair.

Perspective

Along with tone and texture, the use of perspective will give your drawings added authenticity with a sense of depth and distance. Don't be put off by the technicalities; when you understand the basic principles, you can train yourself to 'see' perspective with an artist's eye.

Drawing to convey depth and distance through perspective doesn't mean that you have to become an expert in mathematics. However, initially, it's useful to know a bit about the concept of linear perspective and, if you're working with colour, the ways in which we perceive light for aerial or atmospheric perspective. Once you understand and can implement the theories, you will be able to apply them more intuitively.

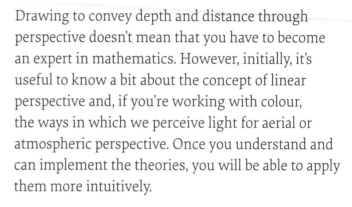

The picture plane

This is an imaginary plane corresponding to the surface of a picture. It is everything that appears to be on the surface of a work of art, but without any depth. If you imagine viewing whatever you are drawing through a sheet of acrylic glass, then tracing exactly what you see on the glass, you will get a two-dimensional representation known as the picture plane.

It is important to be aware of the picture plane when drawing, because if you place objects in your foreground – on the picture plane – you can use them as a marker when putting objects in the middle and background, to create a sense of perspective.

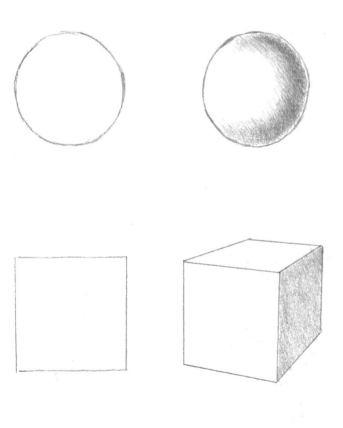

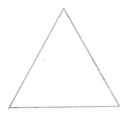

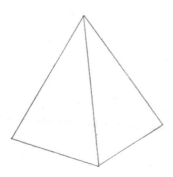

Some initial ideas and tips

As objects recede, or go into the distance, they appear to become smaller. These changes in scale can be barely imperceptible if the background objects are not far away or are huge, which can seem illogical. Things also appear to be closer together as they recede. If you are drawing from life, assess these changes in scale and distance using the sight-sizing (thumb and pencil proportion) measuring technique explained on page 34. This will help you to measure their relative sizes, distances apart and edges. Also, as discussed on page 33, to achieve accurate proportions you need to look at relationships between sizes of objects and spaces within them. Thus, wherever and whenever you think of it, compare height and size ratios with everything you are drawing, if possible. For example,

how many times does the length of a building or a tree go into the width of your landscape? How many times would that orange fit into that jug? By constantly measuring relative heights of and distances between things and making indications with a few light lines, you will make sure that your drawing looks spatially correct. It might take time at first, but it will become second nature soon.

Another tip that can be helpful, especially when you're starting out with perspective, is to draw yourself a border before you begin a drawing. Just a rectangle on your paper like a frame, and work within it. This is helpful for both linear perspective and composition, as it gives you a clear edge to work towards and within, and it will help to concentrate your mind on keeping things to scale.

Linear perspective

The basic premise of linear perspective is that things in the distance appear smaller than those in closer proximity. Thus, as you move away from an object or scene, it appears to diminish, and all lines, including parallel lines that go away from you, appear to converge at a vanishing point on the horizon. In life, we see all this and accept it. By showing this in drawings, you will create a convincing illusion of three dimensions. Here is a simplified drawing to illustrate linear perspective.

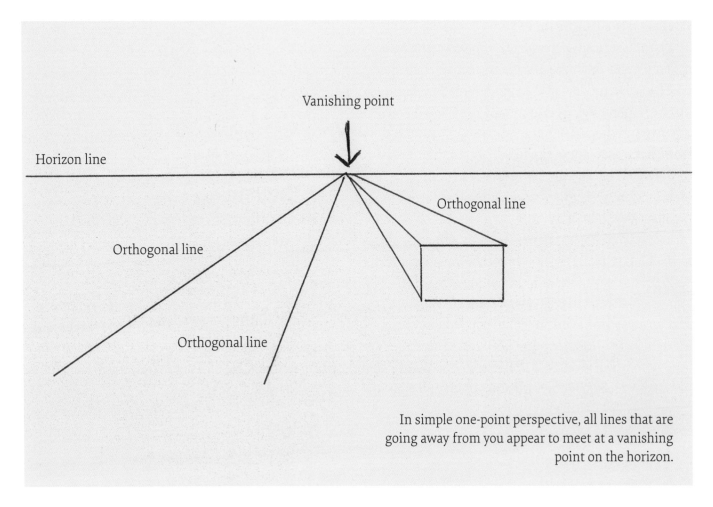

In simple one-point perspective, all lines that are going away from you appear to meet at a vanishing point on the horizon.

Perspective drawing techniques have been used for thousands of years to illustrate three dimensions on flat surfaces. In drawing, we generally use two main forms of linear perspective: one-point and two-point. There are more, including three-point, bird's-eye view and worm's-eye view, which can be used to great effect, but they are strictly for the extremely confident. Linear perspective affects only receding lines, not horizontal, straight ones that are parallel to the picture plane. Certain terms are used in perspective that may seem confusing, so here is a quick run-down:

- **Eye level** is the same level as the horizon. It is the height at which your eyes are when you are looking at and drawing your subject matter.
- **Horizon** is always at eye level and is the line where the sky meets the ground or sea.

- **Converging lines** are parallel lines that appear to merge as they go away from you because of the visual effects of perspective. They are also called **orthogonal lines** or **orthogonals**.
- **Vanishing points** are where the parallel lines appear to meet – and vanish – on the horizon.

We can't always see the vanishing point in an image – for example, it may be through a wall – but when you are honing your skills in the technique make a light mark for it on your paper as a guide. You can use a ruler or your pencil to follow the lines that appear to go away from you, and where they converge, or would converge if they continued, is your vanishing point.

ONE-POINT PERSPECTIVE

The simplest form of perspective – one-point, also called parallel or single-point perspective – is when objects converge towards a single vanishing point on the horizon line. It is generally used when you are viewing the subject matter directly from the front, such as looking directly down a straight road or railway track or into the centre of a room. Interior architects and designers often adopt this form of perspective when drawing their plans. Surfaces that face you, or are flat on to you – that is, are horizontal to the picture plane – remain as they are, with no changes or distortions. Objects of the same size appear smaller as they go away from you, and lines that go away from you appear to converge towards a single vanishing point that is directly ahead of you, at your eye level. So a drawing in one-point perspective has just one vanishing point and is used

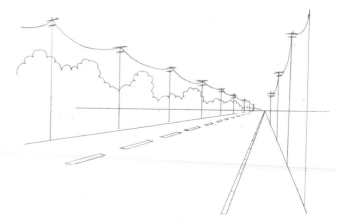

only when you are looking directly, flat-on to the centre of your subject matter.

Boxes

The boxes below are drawn in one-point perspective. Notice the vanishing point and how the receding lines change, depending on where the boxes are in relation to that. Also observe how the vertical and horizontal lines don't change.

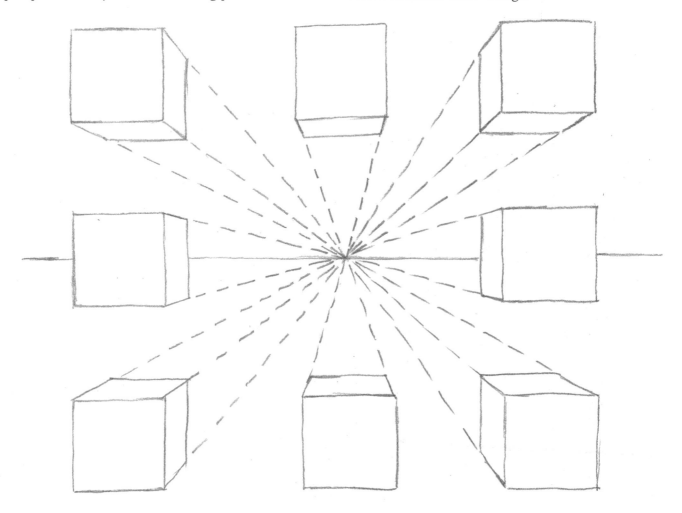

Through the woods

This on-the-spot sketch of a path through a wood incorporates several of the things we have already discussed in this book, including making scribbled marks to depict texture and tone It also shows that linear perspective does not have to rely on rulers and precise drawing. The vanishing point is beyond the trees.

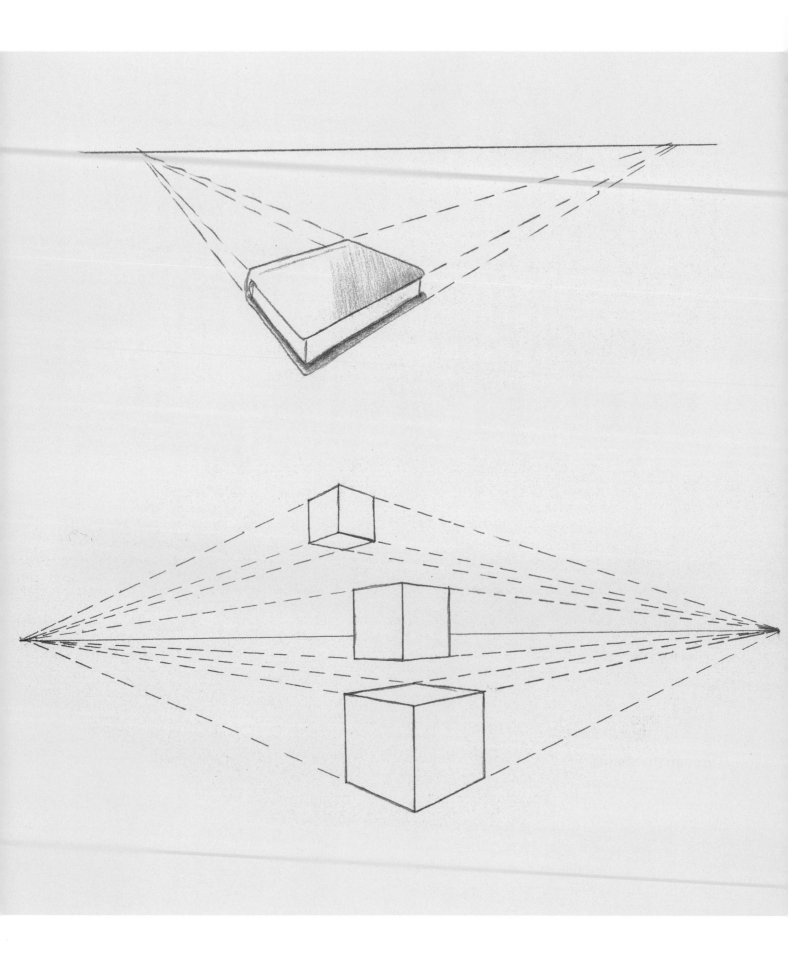

TWO-POINT PERSPECTIVE

Use two-point perspective when drawing something that is not facing you directly but has a corner near to you, or you are standing slightly to the side of it. This is the most common type of linear perspective in drawing, and instead of one vanishing point in the middle there are two, both at eye level, usually either side of your picture or scene. Often, the two vanishing points will occur off the edges of your paper.

Book and boxes

The book and boxes on page 46 are drawn in two-point perspective. Notice the vanishing points are on either side, not necessarily evenly spaced, and the receding lines go towards them.

House

This drawing of a house (below) is in two-point perspective with a low viewpoint. The vanishing points are beyond the edges of the page.

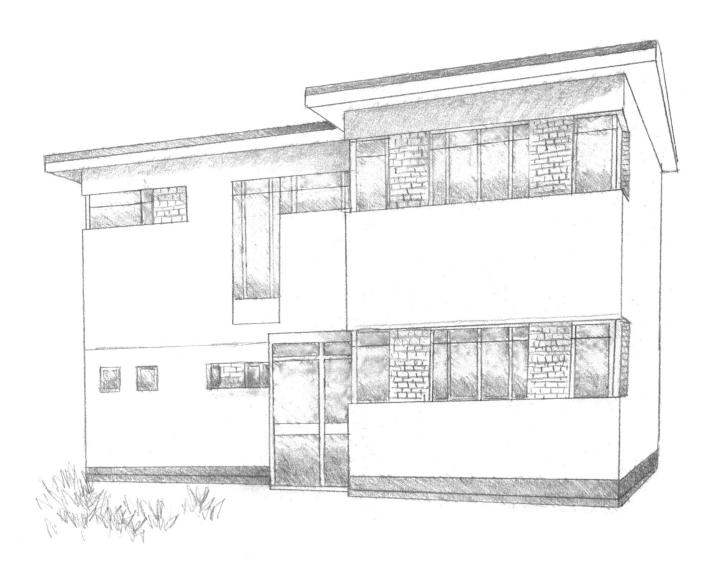

Aerial or atmospheric perspective

A method of creating the illusion of depth and distance in pictures or drawings through colour is called aerial or atmospheric perspective. It is a way of suggesting distance by showing the effects of atmosphere on the landscape, making distances mistier, more blue-grey and less distinct than the foreground. Leonardo da Vinci first used the terms 'aerial perspective' and 'the perspective of disappearance' in his notebooks that were later published as his *Treatise on Painting* in the 16th century. He wrote: 'Colours become weaker in proportion to their distance from the person who is looking at them.' It has since been proved scientifically, because moisture and tiny particles of dust passing through the atmosphere cause light to scatter, and the amount of this scattering corresponds to the colour of the light. Blue light has the shortest wavelength and is scattered most, so distant colours appear bluer or bluish. Any matter in the air, from dust to raindrops to snow, will block the light bouncing off an object, limiting what

reaches the eye. Even on a relatively clear day, the accumulation of atmospheric density can signal to the viewer that one object is farther away than another. Without regard to the linear perspective of a scene, the clarity of lines and surfaces alone can suggest their relative position in space, but when used together linear and aerial perspective can produce convincing illusions of space and dimension. To create the appearance of aerial perspective, make faaway colours lighter, mistier and more blue-grey than those in close-up, and also define distant objects with less detail than those nearby.

The Thames Below Westminster

This pencil sketch (below) is based loosely on a painting by Claude Monet (1840–1926) called *The Thames Below Westminster* of 1871. It is simply to show you how to achieve aerial perspective in pencil. Note how the background is vaguely drawn while the foreground is bolder.

Foreshortening

Foreshortening was first studied during the 15th century by artists in northern Italy, including Francesco Squarcione (1395–1468) and Andrea Mantegna (1431–1506). Like linear and aerial perspective, foreshortening is an optical illusion. Objects appear larger in comparison to other things in a picture or scene because they are close to us, but foreshortening makes this effect appear as a distortion, such as a hand coming towards us. In comparison to the rest of the body, the hand will seem huge. The illusion of foreshortening is created by these close-up objects appearing larger and more compressed than they are in reality, and it occurs in anything you draw, from buildings to landscapes, still lifes to figures, if you are viewing them in close-up. For example if you are drawing a man lying on his back with his feet facing you, his feet will appear far larger than his head. Or if you are drawing a cup with the handle fairly close to you, the handle will appear inordinately big. The more dramatic the perspective, the more distinct the foreshortening will be.

A foreshortened hand

The man above reaching out shows foreshortening in action. His hand and arm seem deformed because of the way they are coming towards us.

3

You should still be looking more at your subject matter than your drawing, which may sound awkward but it works. Only look at your drawing to make sure that you are drawing in the right places. Take your time and establish tonal contrasts across the image. See the dark tones as shapes on each object.

4

Build up the tones and adjust any outlines as you work. Erase any pencil smudges or over-zealous shading. See where the darkest areas are, and where these grow lighter gently or suddenly. Notice that highlights are pure white on parts of some of the fruits and leave the paper showing through here. Observe the dark line and some shading 'anchoring' the bottom of the jug, the orange, pear and one grape to the ground.

Composition

So far, most of the ideas and exercises in this book have been about drawing shapes, patterns, perspective and tonal contrasts. Composition is about putting it all together.

Composition describes the arrangement of elements in an image, and deciding where to put individual elements of a drawing is an important part of being an accomplished artist. A strong and visually pleasing image draws viewers' eyes in and around the image, and there are many ways to accomplish this.

The importance of planning

Compositions can be symmetrical or asymmetrical, top- or bottom-heavy, busy or empty, but whatever they are they all begin with a starting point – the artist's vision or idea before he or she begins drawing. Yes, you can just start drawing and add things here and there as you go along, but it is far better for the final result if you have planned at least where the most important elements of your drawing will be placed before you begin.

Good design enhances a drawing's effectiveness. It involves deciding how big or small to make things, what shapes to use, what to emphasize, where to place objects, how strong to make tonal contrasts, where light is coming from, what details and textures to include and what you want viewers to focus their attention on. Also important is what to leave out of a composition. But this does not have to be complex. There are simple ways to enhance your compositions, and you can make each as easy or as unfussy as you prefer. Once you've read through this chapter, and perhaps had a chance to notice what makes a good composition in some famous works of art, make some thumbnail sketches, working out where you will put objects in your intended drawing. Consider things such as viewpoint, whether or not you will be close in, as well as any of the hints, tips and suggestions mentioned here.

Some elements of composition

Certain elements will make a difference to any composition. They include the following.

Lines lead viewers' eyes in and around the drawing, or send them elsewhere. Lines can be literal, such as the edges of a road or building, or suggested, such as empty spaces between objects. Angular, broken or curving lines can suggest movement, while horizontal lines can create tension or imply tranquillity. Strong, vertical lines often give the impression of height and grandeur.

Shapes are areas defined by edges, and whether geometric or organic they help to create the overall 'feeling' of every drawing. Shapes are made with lines, shading, colours and/or negative spaces. Simplification of shapes and outlines can help to make drawings easy to read.

Colour, whether soft, pale, deep or bright, can have a powerful effect on compositions, depending on their intensity and placement, while colour symbolism adds additional associations, depending on culture. Choose your colours carefully: for example, bold colours catch attention; cool ones can appear to recede; and colours juxtaposed with their complementary ones will appear even brighter. Using the same or similar colours can draw the eye to particular parts of a composition.

Textured surface qualities that translate into tactile illusions also affect compositions.

Value and contrast will affect the overall appearance of a drawing, if shading is strong (as in chiaroscuro) or soft (as in sfumato). The tonal placement – including where light falls – will also make a difference to your composition. Darker areas in a predominantly light drawing will stand out and draw the eye, and the same happens for the reverse. So tonal contrast should be used to focus

attention. Make sure you are not adding emphasis that draws away from where you intend your main focal point to be.

Spaces between objects (negative space) can either pull a composition together, or not, and depending on their size and placement they can change an entire drawing's composition.

Focal point describes the main centre of interest in a drawing; it is the place where viewers' eyes are naturally drawn. Try to decide on what your focal point will be before you start drawing.

Balance, also sometimes called unity, helps all compositions. This does not mean that everything has to be symmetrical, but the arrangement has to appear stable.

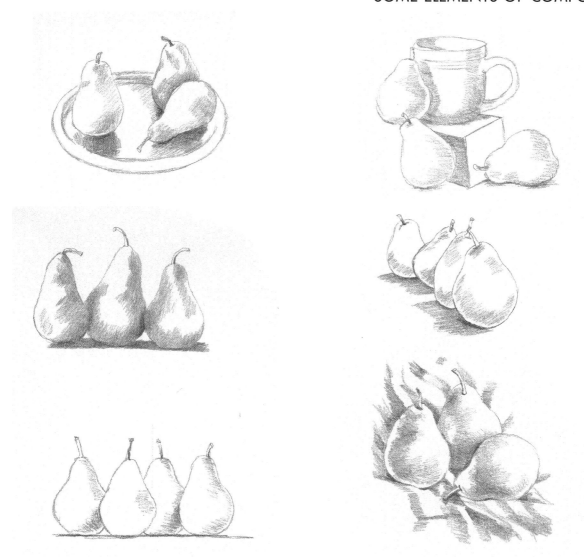

Proportion refers to the dimensions of the various components of a drawing, and is important in composition. The subject matter can be rendered more dramatic when it fills the frame, but even if you're not aiming for drama you should resist the temptation to draw tiny objects. Fill your space by making things as large as you can, because the larger you draw them the more impact they will have, and also it will be easier to include tonal and textural marks. This will also eliminate distractions from the background.

Rhythm can be created with patterns, lines, tonal contrast, repetition and/or colour and helps to ease viewers' eyes across and around a composition.

Viewpoint can influence how a drawing is judged. Thus, depending on the perceived position of viewers, a drawing can seem dramatic, calm, immediate or something completely different. Think of bird's eye, worm's eye, a view from dramatic close up, or long distance.

Although the thumbnails of pears (above) are small and simplified, they explore some of these ideas on composition and are just here to show you how different elements of composition work. They also demonstrate how, although there are these universal ideas or even 'rules' about composition, everyone has different ideas about what works; it's really a quite individual reaction to what they see in front of them.

Some helpful tips

Every picture should have some point of interest. Sometimes this is simply a spot of light or colour. Or it may be a face, a tree or a tall building. Here are some ideas to get you started:

- Group objects together and include some overlap, because this creates depth and a sense of reality.
- Draw objects in odd rather than even numbers for a stronger composition, and don't be too formal or precise with their placement; anything too exact or matching will seem unlikely and can appear boring. It has been shown that an odd number of objects in an image is more interesting than an even number, which often creates a symmetrical image and can appear less natural for a naturalistic, informal composition.
- Some objects look more convincing if they seem to go off the edge of the drawing.
- Sometimes, when you've completed a picture, use a viewfinder – two paper or card corners made into a frame – to see what your image would look like with cropped edges. In this way, you can create focus on its interest and possibly make the entire composition more 'immediate'.
- Objects should not face out of the composition: for example, a jug's spout or a face in profile should face inwardly.
- Unusual or unexpected viewpoints can be compelling, as can cropping any unnecessary elements; even sky may be superfluous in some pictures.

The good news is that every one of these ideas can be totally ignored. They work for most images, but by no means all, and many drawings look good without applying any of these ideas at all. So it's fine to challenge the rules.

Compositional arrangements

Don't let the following confuse you or put you off. Most good ideas about composition are instinctive, and you'll find that when you are satisfied you will probably also satisfy your viewers. It is useful, however, to be aware of a few things that can enhance the overall look and compel viewers to scan the most important parts immediately, or to observe everything in the correct order. Compelling compositions use a number of techniques that artists have tried and tested through the ages. Here are a few.

X shape

Focusing elements in the centre of the composition, leads the eyes into the image. The X-shaped composition is often an example of one-point perspective (see page 44).

+ shape

A cross-shaped composition can be quite versatile, but it's best to position the main image to one side. The horizon line can be high or low, and the vertical intersection to the right or left, but always to the side of the centre for most interest.

Y shape

This composition usually focuses on one main element such as a tree or a person. A painting of 1870–73 by William Holman Hunt (1827–1910) called *The Shadow of Death* is a particularly powerful version of this kind of composition.

Rule of thirds

Compositions divided into thirds horizontally and vertically are almost always visually pleasing. In this way, nothing in the drawing, whether the horizon or any object, will bisect the image. A composition in thirds is fairly straightforward to achieve. Base it loosely on a grid; imagine overlaying the grid for a game of noughts and crosses on your drawing, so your image is split into thirds, horizontally and vertically. Place your main subject matter or focal point somewhere along those grid lines. This format is also close to the classical 'golden section'.

Triangular

A classical portrait or group is often in a triangular composition. Think of Leonardo da Vinci's *Mona Lisa*

S shape
The curving line leading into and through a picture is compelling for all artists and viewers.

L shape
By creating a natural 'lever' shape, you are framing your drawing on one side and thus containing the main elements within that shape, which compels viewers to concentrate on them. An L shape also offers space on one side of the picture, which helps to draw viewers' eyes into the focal point and thus can create a sense of depth within the composition.

O shape
A calm, serene composition is especially effective within an O shape. Although not as common as many of the other shapes, it can be powerful, creating a frame within a frame. The c.1653–6 painting *Diana and Her Companions* by Johannes Vermeer (1632–75) is a strong example of a O-shaped composition.

THEMES

The best way to develop your drawing skills is through directly observing things and drawing what you see, looking at the subject more than your drawing and remaining objective. Check negative shapes, squinting to establish tonal values and measuring with your pencil. Once you have followed the exercises and examples in this book, try drawing imaginary objects as well as some from direct observation. Begin with simple, organic objects such as apples, tomatoes or peppers, and build up to something like folded fabric, box-like shapes, plants, landscapes or a pet. The man-made environment, portraits and figures may seem more challenging at first, but they are all basically the same – just shapes, angles and tones. You'll be amazed at what you can achieve once you have some fundamental confidence in your own ability. When you learnt to read and write, and if you've ever learnt to drive a car, remember how you felt at first – daunted, perhaps? It was going to be difficult and challenging, but you mastered it. It's the same with drawing. Take time to really look closely at everything, constantly notice the things we have discussed, including tonal contrasts and their depth and placement, light sources, the strength or weakness of this light, relative sizes, angles and proportions. Look for vanishing points, practise making different patterns and marks to show texture. How will you show movement? How can you draw the effects of light and weather?

The following part of the book shows you how to put everything together. It is divided into themes: still life, landscapes, animals, portraits and figures, and in each chapter there are examples and detailed step-by-step projects. Have a go at some or all of them. Remain positive – don't tell yourself what you can't do – remind yourself constantly what you are able to achieve. No matter how unsure you might feel, if you can write your name, you can draw; if you can make different marks with a pencil or pen, you can draw. The more you draw, the more you will improve. Take your time, be patient, and try some of the following projects.

Still life

Still lifes are great to draw because they can comprise anything you can find, and they stay still. Drawing still life compositions can help you develop the most invaluable, basic skills.

The term 'still life' comes from the Dutch *stil leven*, meaning the 'representation of a motionless aspect of nature'. This makes it great for learning how to draw, teaching you how to look at objects with a perceptive awareness of their outlines, shapes, proportions, tones, colours, textures, forms and composition. Every element of still life arrangements can be manipulated, enabling you to strengthen your skills in setting up compositions, drawing assorted shapes and adding tone and texture to evoke the appearance of reality. Still life objects will change only if you are including things such as vegetables, fruit or flowers over several weeks. If you have little drawing experience, choose

objects with simple, basic shapes. More advanced artists can make arrangements of objects of any size, shape and detail level that suits their skills.

This chapter will help you draw still lifes, giving you ideas to improve your drawing techniques and approaches, and suggestions for materials and subject matter. The techniques, methods and skills are transferable to all kinds of drawing, and everything described in this book will also be helpful: for example, making textural marks, building tonal contrasts, looking for negative spaces, and working out perspective and composition.

If you are just starting out, try drawing single items initially. There are several here and on previous pages. Pick an apple, a cup, a glass or a book, for example, then build up to simple arrangements of ordinary, everyday objects such as a spoon and knife, a box of cereal and a bowl, a ball and cricket bat, or a flower pot and a trowel. Notice how the objects shown above – the shells, spoon and knife, rose, tomato. grapes and strawberry – have fairly simple, rounded outlines.

Once the shapes have been established, most of your time should be spent on the shading, to make each one look three-dimensional.

Grouping objects

It's always best to use objects that complement or are related to each other, such as groups of kitchen utensils, toys, gardening tools or shells. However, this is entirely up to you; whatever you want to draw is fine, whether the objects are usually seen together or not.

When arranging your chosen objects, think of ways you will visually link them; perhaps they are touching or appearing to overlap as they are in front of each other, or maybe shadows hold them together. Try arranging the objects by adding or removing items randomly, until you are happy with the arrangement and feel confident that you can draw it. Consider the background; this may be important as part of the composition, or you may choose not to include one. Sometimes, a piece of fabric or a draped curtain can visually pull everything together. Think about contrasts, as well as similarities. Will a dark or light background, plain or patterned, textured or smooth backdrop enhance or detract from your arrangement?

Here are some drawings of a variety of objects, including a ballpoint-pen depiction of a wine bottle and glass – notice the overlap of objects and the strong contrasts of dark and light to represent shine; a pencil drawing of a parlour palm; and a jug and peach, which are drawn in pencil, with pencil for the peach. I used a sketch-like approach for the palm – not every leaf or detail is included. Although the jug and peach do not overlap, they are pulled together visually by the echoing peach – the actual object and its reflections in the shiny, silver jug.

Still life subjects

Still life can be of any inanimate object you choose.
So group together things from the sport you play,
your hobby (such as sewing, gardening or cooking)
or other things that interest you (such as cakes,
flowers, toys, clocks or compasses – or even shoes).

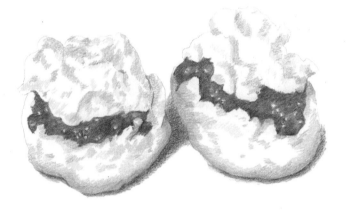

Initial tips

Thumbnails

As shown in the chapter on composition (see page 58), thumbnails can be useful when you are setting up a still life. Alternatively, take a few photos to check the compositions. These will give you the chance to consider several compositional options before committing to any particular one.

Simplifying shapes

Reducing objects to simple shapes can help you to draw the arrangement with some accuracy, and allow you to observe the perspective more clearly.

Using a viewfinder

Once you have set up a composition, use a viewfinder to decide on the format of your drawing. When a picture is taller than it is wide, it is known as being in portrait format, while a picture that is wider than it is tall is described as being in landscape format. For your viewfinder, make a framing device out of two L shapes cut from a piece of card. Hold them up as a frame and look through it to see how close in you should crop your drawing.

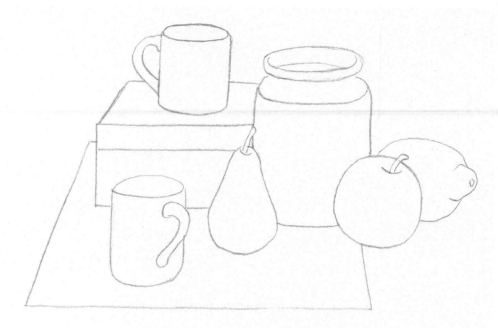

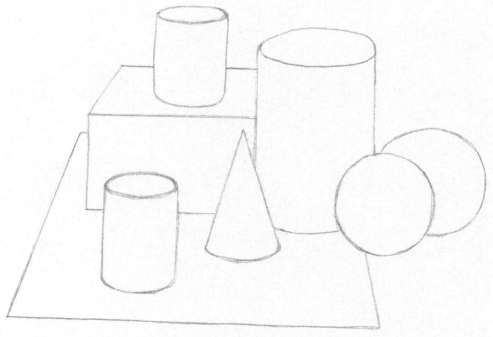

Measuring

Use the pencil technique shown on page 34 to build up a network of measurements and proportions for all the objects in your still life.

Light source

Try to have one main light source for your still life as this will help with light and shade.

MATERIALS: CARTRIDGE PAPER, B AND 2B PENCILS, ERASER, COLOURED PENCILS

Fruit

For the first step-by-step still life, select uncomplicated objects with simple shapes, such as fruit or vegetables, or mugs, jars or boxes. I've used an apple, orange, pear, lemon, three bananas and two cherries on a wooden board. The board helps to hold each piece of fruit together in the composition, and its viewpoint is from slightly above, looking down, rather than the more usual one that would look across at the items. Set up your objects on a flat surface that is near a comfortable seat. Ideally, choose a place with some form of natural light or near a good lamp.

1

2

Draw the outline of the board, as this will be the 'anchor' for the drawing and will make sure you keep within the space you have for the entire drawing.

Using the B pencil, draw a large circle shape (although here it is slightly imperfect) for the orange in the background, and begin to draw the gently curving banana on its side to the left of the orange. Keep looking at the whole arrangement to see the shapes and spaces between each object. Draw lightly so that if you have to erase any marks you won't leave any dark marks or indentations.

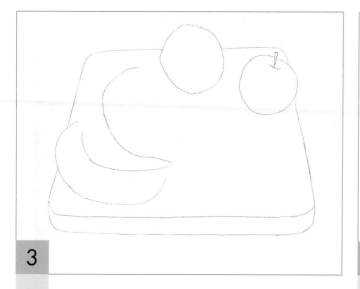

3

Measure and check lines and angles with your pencil. Keep looking at the objects, more than at your drawing; check perspective lines, spaces and shapes between each piece of fruit. Draw the rounded outline of the apple and its stalk.

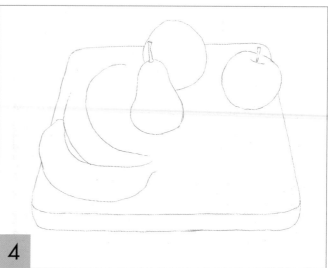

4

Now add the pear. It's a triangular shape in front of the circular orange. Note the sizes of the space between these two and the apple.

5

Draw the outline of the lemon and two cherries. Notice the overlap between the orange, pear and lemon, while the bananas touch the pear, and the apple and cherries are separate from them all, slightly to one side of the board. Check all the angles and shapes. Erase any superfluous lines and make sure everything looks accurate as you will be adding shading next.

6

Half-close your eyes to see the darkest tones and what shapes they are. Using the 2B pencil, begin to build up your shading, using a light touch. Layer the shading so that in shadowed areas you cover any white areas of paper showing through, but leave highlighted areas white and untouched. The deeper tones, such as next to the pieces of fruit on the left-hand side, need to be built up with slightly firmer pressure and more layers, but don't press too hard. Work across the picture and notice how and where the shadows and darker tones help to pull everything together.

7

Continue to build up the shading, observing where light falls; don't be heavy-handed. Here, there is reflected light and direct light, as well as cast shadows. Try to include a full range of values to make your drawing look more realistic. When you are almost finished, put the picture to one side for at least a day, or else hold it up to a mirror. In either case, you will see it with fresh eyes, and any mistakes will become apparent. Adjust those and also, if you have been over-zealous with your shading, use an eraser or putty eraser to 'lift out' the brightest highlights.

8

Try drawing the same arrangement with coloured pencils. No black has been used in this drawing; the darkest tones are made with mixtures of dark grey, dark blue or dark brown.

Gardens

If you have a garden, this can be
a great place to start landscape
drawing. If not, can you access a
local park or communal garden?
The best way to draw is always from
direct observation, but if you are self-
conscious and prefer not to draw in
public, take photographs and work
when you get home. Draw simple
elements to begin with: for example,
a bench or plants on a patio; a trellis
with a climbing rose; an array of
hollyhocks; or a path to a front or back
door. Then try drawing brick walls,
ponds, birds, flowers, a bird feeder or
a shed.

Trees

Other useful elements to practise separately for landscape drawing are trees, as in general trees form a vital part of the landscape. You may simply want to draw them as the merest impressions, but it is useful to know how to reproduce their form and structure.

Trees are usually seen against a light sky, which makes them appear darker than they are, and lower branches are shaded by those above. Notice how branches are not usually particularly curving but have an angularity, and several will be foreshortened as they come towards you. Cast shadows of trees can help to describe the irregularity of the surface they fall on, such as rough stone, long grass or a noticeable slope. All varieties of trees have characteristic overall shapes, such as cone-shaped fir trees, umbrella-shaped maples and oaks and elegantly structured silver birches.

With all trees, begin by drawing the trunk. Then add the branches. These grow up and out towards the sun and are thicker at the base and thinner at the ends. Don't try to draw every individual leaf, but instead concentrate on the general outline of the area taken up by them. Observe an entire tree with half-closed eyes, to eliminate details and only identify broad areas of light and shade. No tree is symmetrical, and shading is crucial to add the illusion of depth and dimension. Once you have decided where the main light source is coming from, begin to build up the tones. To add shading

to the leaves, apply short, straight lines or circular, scribble-like marks. The scribble-type action is particularly effective for leaves because of the effect of texture this imparts, and is especially useful if you build up small clusters and leave some empty spaces around them.

Buildings

To include some of the man-made environment in your landscape, think about its composition, because the amount of space taken up with buildings, where they are and how large or prominent they are in your drawing are all important considerations. Will the buildings be obscured by trees or softened by some sort of other foliage, or is your drawing to be a town- or cityscape? Even a country scene can have added interest with one or two well-placed buildings or objects such as street lamps, post boxes, brick walls or church spires, for example. These can act as stabilizers for the picture or focal points, leading viewers' eyes into and around the image.

When you have chosen your buildings, look at them from various angles, from near and far, and at different times of day. That way you will see shadows, angles and complex elements before you start drawing. Be careful with the perspective and, using your entire arm, draw your own straight lines rather than use a ruler (unless you are doing a technical drawing). They are worth practising and will become easier.

Water

Like the sky, clouds and trees, water is often an important element in a landscape, so practise drawing the still water of lakes, ponds, and lagoons, moving streams or rivers and waves crashing against rocks. Although water is transparent, large expanses have different colours, either reflected from above and around them, or filtering through from beneath, from the seabed, or from minerals, rocks or algae. The reflective quality is most noticeable when water is still. When drawing it, consider your materials carefully, as tonal techniques are more effective for water than linear ones. Add in any reflections or highlights last of all.

Bringing everything together

In general, a landscape drawing is wider than it is high, but how you organize it depends on your subject and composition. Some landscape subject matters look better in portrait format. Of course, you may abandon the rectangle shape altogether and draw on a square or even circular format.

Before you begin a composition, consider which elements you will include. For example, will you have an expanse of open sky, and will you be able to see the foreground, middle ground and background clearly? As already considered in the book (see page 48), the background should contain fewer details than the foreground, and not much tone because of the effects of aerial perspective, while the foreground has the most detail with the strongest suggestion of tone and texture.

MATERIALS: CARTRIDGE PAPER, B, 2B AND 5B PENCILS, ERASER

Spring day

This is a view of a spring day, looking directly through some trees in one-point perspective, to create an illusion of three-dimensional space. Before you begin sketching any landscape, determine the position of your horizon line as it divides the space between the land and sky.

1

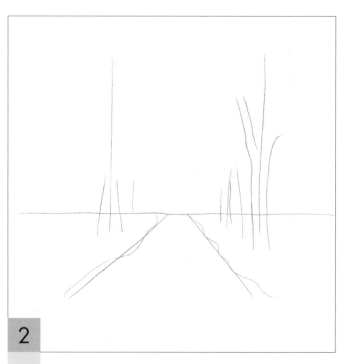

2

Using the B pencil, make a horizon line your first mark on the paper. Draw lightly with your pencil so you can erase any mistakes or other marks, if necessary. Then draw the path and a couple of vertical lines to indicate roughly where the path emerges through the trees, and to position a couple of the tree trunks.

Soften the outer lines of the path and begin to add shape to the trees closest to the viewer. They will be the largest objects in the landscape, while the rest of the trees, grass and sky will have less definition as they are farther away.

3 Begin to build up the trees on either side of the path, ensuring they are smaller as they recede. The original vertical lines should be used as guides for placement of these trees. Erase any marks you no longer need – this is why it's so important not to press hard with your pencil.

4 Add more branches and make them stretch over the path. These should not be too curving or sinuous, but slightly angular. Also, start to draw the fence posts behind the trees. Some can tilt slightly in different directions, but keep perspective in mind as you draw them.

5

Now using the 2B pencil, begin to create leaves by using squiggle-type marks, building up the overall mass of foliage rather than defining individual leaves. Some branches can be seen through the leaves. Also carry on drawing the fence posts and add a slight hint of cast shadow under the trees.

6

Continue creating the appearance of leaves in the trees, using both the 2B and 5B pencils, and also start to join the fence posts and build up some of the tones and textures on the tree trunks. As the light is coming from above, the cast shadows appear on both sides of the path, but don't shade smoothly; little vertical marks can create the appearance of grass on the banks.

7

To produce the effects of aerial perspective, add light marks at the end of the path to suggest more trees in the distance. Don't give these outlines; they should be vague. Elsewhere, carry on building up the textural marks on the darkest parts of the trees and on some leaves – this is a spring day, so the leaves are only just growing back on the branches. Add more tufts of grass here and there, leaving some white space.

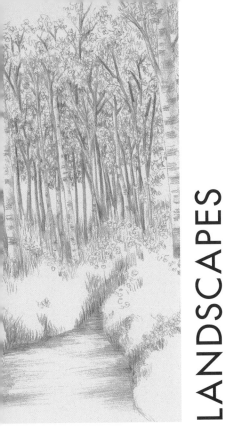

MATERIALS: CARTRIDGE PAPER, B, 2B AND 5B PENCILS, ERASER; PLUS, FOR THE COLOURED PENCIL VERSION: COLOURED PENCILS IN LIGHT BROWN, DARK BROWN, GREY, DARK BLUE, LIGHT BLUE, PINK, YELLOW AND GREEN

Woodland

This is another view of trees but in a more dense forest than in the previous project. The birch trees here are slender, with contrasting marks on their trunks.

1

As the trees are clustered together in this scene, begin by marking on some roughly vertical lines to indicate where some of the trees will stand. Use the B pencil for this. As a guide, and to keep the composition centred on the paper, also lightly mark on the area that leads into the grass – such an 'arrow' will point to the main part of the drawing and subconsciously attract viewers' eyes.

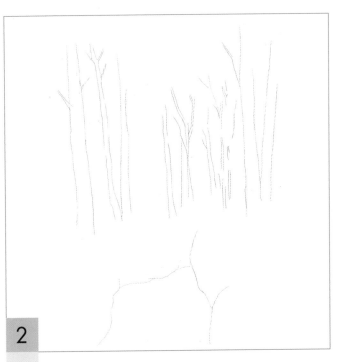

2

Firm up the 'arrow' of land at the front, then start to draw in some more definite tree trunks. The outer trunks are wider than the central ones, because of perspective; they are closer to viewers than the trees in the centre.

3

Continue drawing the trees. Although tall and thin, none is uniform or symmetrical; all have branches that spread at the top, and each trunk appears to become narrower as it recedes into the distance. You can also introduce some soft, short tufts of grass.

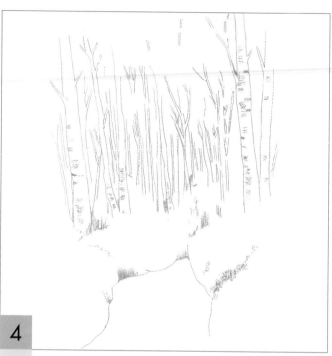

4

Using the 2B pencil, begin drawing marks on the tree trunks. As with the trunks and branches themselves, such marks should be haphazard and asymmetrical because they are organic. Notice too that the trees themselves occupy more than half of the composition.

5

Make sure that your trees overlap in places to show linear perspective, while some parts in the distance will be lighter and less detailed to show aerial perspective. Build up more marks on the trunks, some grass and some cast shadows, always using a light touch.

6

Squint your eyes to see where the light is coming from and apply shadows consistently across the scene. Use the 5B pencil and make sure some trunks and leaves are much darker than the lightest areas. The grass in the foreground is more apparent and carefully drawn than the overall sense of flowers closer to the tree trunks. The narrower trunks appear much darker than the broader ones, as they are in shadow – behind the lighter trunks and under the canopy of leaves.

7

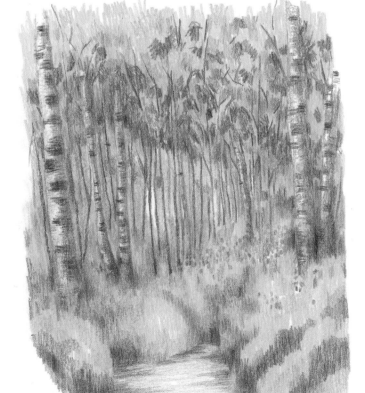

This is the same scene but rendered in coloured pencils. Use loose, tight, long and short marks, plus scribbled-type marks for the leaves and straighter marks for the grass. Also build up contrasting marks on the tree trunks. Intense greens are created through layers, always bearing in mind where the darkest shadows are. Some of the darkest areas of green were made with dark blue and brown layered over green. No black was used, as this can flatten the look of a picture. Because coloured pencils can sometimes be a bit too vivid and unnatural for a landscape, I also added some layers of light grey in places. Be patient; this kind of coloured pencil drawing takes time.

Animals

However lovable they are, animals rarely oblige and pose for you long enough for you to draw them, so try to get into the habit of making quick sketches whenever you see an animal you would like to draw. Mark down only the main simplified shapes of each animal, as shown on page 32. Textures, tones and other details can be added later.

While drawing from life is always best, with such active subjects, photos are a great help so have a camera, mobile phone or tablet to hand, and also use any reference pictures you can find in books or magazines or on the internet. The trouble with photographs is that they can result in fairly static drawings. Also, relying on photographs can sap your confidence; you can become used to them and your ability to observe with that artist's eye can fade. Fortunately, it won't take long to develop it again,

but be aware that, even with animals that are easier captured on camera, jotting down what you observe directly will result in a better sense of life and animation in your drawings.

This chapter will introduce you to drawing a diversity of animals from domestic to wild, small to large, furry to feathered, plain and patterned. Inevitably, it can't be comprehensive, so there are bound to be animals you would like to draw that are not here. Hopefully, however, it will give you the fundamentals of knowing what to look for, what to omit and what to emphasize in any drawing of any animal; also how to make textures, markings, facial features and even movements look realistic. To begin, try drawing a fairly well-known animal such as a cat, dog or rabbit to ascertain where you might find difficulties and what you would like to improve or know more about. Here are a few general things to consider.

Fur, feathers and facial features

Fur and feathers are conveyed through different marks. When drawing them, look for shapes created with light and dark tones, as you did in the landscape chapter with grass, leaves and clouds, for example (see pages 78–91). All animal coats start from various points and grow in different directions, and there are many different strokes you can use when drawing long hair, short hair, curly, wiry fur and light, smooth coats. Much of this requires gentle strokes of different lengths and shapes, plus layering, but you should always draw in the direction of each animal's fur. One of the biggest beginners' mistakes is stopping too soon, giving

up too early, because if you add enough layers in the right places you can build up a sense of credible fur. Both fur and feathers appear different over the curves of an animal or bird's body as they overlap and lie in varying directions.

Notice the features of the animal you are drawing, especially the eyes, which characterize every living creature's face. While all eyes have some similarities, they also have numerous distinct differences. Look carefully to check these features: for example, the size and shape of the nose, mouth, eyes and ears. The pupils and nostrils are usually the darkest parts on any face. As with the skin or coat, sensitive layering will enable you to build up a glow and sense of depth in the eyes, while applying a range of tonal values will help you indicate the smoothness and shine, or otherwise, on all the features of each animal.

Markings

Like fur and feathers, markings or patterns on animals are not uniform. Even if they may look symmetrical, they never are. When you first look at the animal or bird, consider the overall effect as simple shapes and areas of dark and light. Refer to animal textures and patterns on page 27 to understand the different ways of making marks to create a realistic appearance of animal patterning. Also, consider how to show the effects on three-dimensional animals, with all their curves. Variations occur in the tonal values as parts of the animal appear to recede or advance, or are in shadow under bellies, legs, chins or tails, for example. For most markings, begin by drawing a faint outline of the shapes as you see them, to establish their placement and proportions. Notice irregularities, and build them up with the lightest marks initially.

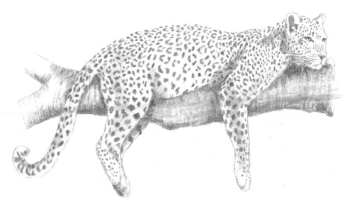

Proportions

Whether you are drawing from photographs or from life, as with all the other subjects in this book so far, observe the proportions of the animal you are drawing and the overall shapes. Notice the negative shapes around the animal, and compare the relative angles and sizes. For example, with this horse, compare the triangular-shaped head with its neck. How many times would the head fit into the body? It's about seven head widths from nose to tail, and about three head lengths from its hooves to the top of its back.

Sketching animals

Pets can be useful animals to draw as you know them and will recognize your own pet's characteristics. Cats, in particular, are great to sketch, as they sleep a lot and make rather graceful shapes. If you have a cat or you know someone who does, catch them in quick outline sketches in pen or pencil on paper while they sleep, using simple lines to capture their fluid shapes. These lines are like shorthand notes. You can do this with any pet, and when you have more time add further marks to build up the appearance of markings and a sense of their fur.

Cats' ears are fairly simple, triangular shapes on their round heads, and their eyes, noses and mouths are fairly close together. They can be drawn in a simplified way, actually joined together. Dogs' bodies are boxier than cats'. Cats are curvy and slinky as a rule, while dogs can often be started with rectangular shapes. Young animals have bigger eyes in comparison with their faces, and different breeds of dog have differently shaped ears, but always shiny noses. Puppies have more rounded heads and bellies than adult dogs. If you don't want to draw domestic animals, you could sketch in a wildlife park, at the zoo or on safari. As with every drawing style and theme we have discussed, your drawing can be realistic only if you observe intensely, turn off your subjective thoughts and be as objective as possible.

Drawing details

Here is a variety of animals, all drawn with different marks to create varying appearances. The West Highland terrier (right) has an outline of curving lines to project the idea of wavy, long, wiry fur. The dalmatian (opposite) has smooth outlines, to convey its short fur, with black spots drawn and shaded, darker in the deeper-toned areas and lighter where the light falls. The tiger (opposite) requires different marks again – short lines, close together for its stripes, with narrow spaces left to show the idea of whiskers. All these three animals have darker marks in shadowed areas and the paper is left showing through, for highlights.

The collie (below) in coloured pencil has differentiated areas within the fur. Fine, flowing, sinuous lines create the sense of soft, wavy fur. Contrastingly, the dolphin (opposite) is rendered smoothly, graduated from light to dark, while clear white lines left between the shading portray shine and wetness. The panther's head (opposite)

is drawn on buff-coloured, parchment-type paper in black ink, which, unlike ballpoint pen or pencil, cannot be lightened with gentler pressure. If you wish to draw an animal in pen and ink, be judicious where you place your marks and where you leave paper showing through. Choose a fine nib and light strokes; the ink should be fluid, but not over-wet. Where you want your lines to taper away, lift your pen. Darken areas with extra lines and layers, while untouched areas suggest light falling on the animal. As with everything else, apply marks with a light touch, and less is more to begin with; you can always add more.

For all materials, whether pencil, pen, coloured pencil, charcoal or any other drawing implement, change your marks – from long to short, or in different directions – depending on the effect you are aiming at, and layer where it will enhance the effects of deeper tones and textures. To prevent overworking an animal drawing, occasionally stop what you are doing and step back. Return to look at it a few hours later, or tomorrow, or even next week, when you will see it with fresh eyes and can be more objective about it. Then, add to it and/or use an eraser to lift any unwanted marks (if the drawing is in pencil), until you are happy with it.

MATERIALS: CARTRIDGE PAPER, B, 2B AND 6B PENCILS, ERASER

ANIMALS

Fluffy cat

This type of fluffy cat can be made to look realistic by making marks in certain areas to show darker tones. There are few individual hairs and strands because of the overall white fluffiness. The fur looks darker where there are shadows and some pale grey markings.

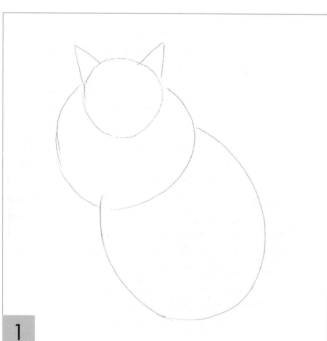

1

Draw simple outline shapes: a circle for the head; another circle for the cat's 'ruff'; and the curving shapes of his body.

2

Mark on the head features, again only in simple shapes, joining them together as shown above. Add the curving tail and the front paw – this cat is sitting sideways on.

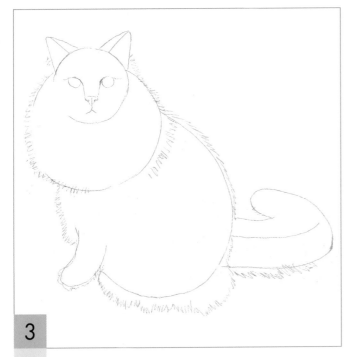

3

Now begin to build up the actual silhouette of the cat, using zigzag, sketchy lines to show the long fur all the way around. As you draw this, begin to erase your earlier guidelines.

4

Continue to erase the initial guidelines, then begin to mark on some areas of long fur. Do this with long pencil strokes and only in places where there are either darker markings on this white cat or where the light does not fall. Continue to enhance the facial features.

5

The long fur requires pencil strokes of differing lengths and darknesses, so use the B and 2B pencils with light pressure. Some of the marks are to show darker tones, and some are to show darker markings. Most of the cat will be left white with no marks at all. Continue to firm up the facial features and add marks under the chin. Work across the whole animal; don't stay in one area for too long, or you will end up with an unbalanced drawing.

6

Use the 6B pencil for the darkest areas on the face, including the pupils, around the eyes and the nostrils. Erase any remaining outlines as you no longer need them and soften any lines that are too dark, by pressing the eraser on them and lifting it off.

7

Complete the drawing by using a soft touch across it and layering the pencil strokes to continue suggesting the long fur. Notice the shine in the eyes – the irises are shaded with the B pencil, which is also used for the softest fur around the face. The 2B is suitable for the slightly deeper-toned areas on the fur, such as under the front paw and in the ears.

MATERIALS: CARTRIDGE PAPER, B AND 3B PENCILS, ERASER

Dalmation puppy

ANIMALS

This puppy is great to draw, especially if you're not feeling particularly confident. Its boxy shape is quite straightforward, and there are only smooth curves to its body.

1

Using the B pencil, lightly draw simplified outline shapes of the puppy – a circular or oval shape for the head, another oval for the shoulder area, a rectangle for the body, and lines to indicate the position and length of the legs.

2

Using your simple shapes as guidelines, begin to build on the outline of the puppy, concentrating on the curves and widths of the legs, the gentle curve of the back, the chest, oval snout and triangular ears. Mark on the curving tail.

3

Continue refining those earlier basic outline shapes into lifelike forms: soften the ears; mark on the eyes, nose and mouth; complete the tail; and start to create the paws and toes.

4

Erase any remaining original guidelines, then continue to adjust the outline – still with the B pencil. Also start to draw on the spots. Notice how they are not regular or perfectly rounded. There are two approaches for this: draw the shape of each mark lightly and then colour it in; or else shade lightly, with little lines or scribble-like marks in the shapes with no outlines. Notice how I adjusted the mouth. In step 3, it was a simplified, almost diagrammatic mouth, here I've made it more naturalistic. Add dark spots for the nostrils.

5

Using the 3B pencil, continue drawing the dog's markings, making sure that some are darker than others, depending on where the light falls. Mark on a tiny circle in each eye – this will be the highlight to make each one look shiny. Also add a little light shading in folds of the skin and ears.

6

For the last stage of the drawing, refine and refine again. Add any last marks and draw in features such as the pupils and irises, and the nose – including nostrils and shading, leaving a white patch to imply shine. Then go back to the B pencil and, with it, add extremely light shading around areas such as the belly and back legs. In general, younger animals require lighter shading than adults.

Once you have drawn that puppy, have a go at the beagle (right). Work in the same way, building up from basic, simple shapes and gradually refining them. Notice that the outline is not particularly complicated, but the shading needs a sensitive touch. Take your time, build up the intensity of darks you see, through layering, and if you feel comfortable with it use a softer pencil – only be aware that softer pencils can smudge. You may find it helpful to place a spare piece of paper under your hand as you draw, to limit this, and then clean up the drawing with an eraser once you have finished.

Portraits

Drawing a portrait is like drawing almost anything. You have to closely observe the subject matter in order to represent it accurately. Of course, portraits can be all sorts of things, not necessarily a realistic rendering of someone's appearance, but here we're talking about conventional drawings of people's faces and, sometimes, figures as well.

Conventional portrait drawing is especially delicate because the goal is to make it look like the human subject and, whether you know the model or not, his or her personality may affect your view. Even if you are being as objective as possible, sitters themselves often don't see themselves as they really are. Some of the most experienced portrait artists have had the same problems. John Singer Sargent (1856–1925) once complained that most of his sitters asked for some feature to be altered, especially the mouth. This prompted him to define a portrait as: 'a likeness in which there is something wrong about the mouth'. As this referred to his refusal to alter anything, he declared: 'Every time I paint a portrait, I lose a friend.'

Often, when you are drawing a portrait, things begin to look a little wrong but you can't define exactly what this is. Usually, it's a combination of issues. Slightly wrong angles or shading in the wrong places, for example. When you are starting out, the main things to focus on are close observation, measurements of angles, shapes, negative spaces and tonal contrasts, and soon those elusive true likenesses will happen.

Proportions of the head

As discussed on pages 38 and 39 in the chapter on space and proportion, there are certain common dimensions in all human heads, although these vary slightly between men, women and children, and between adults of different ages. The following provides a few more guidelines that you can use to check the general size, shape and position of elements of faces when doing a portrait drawing:

• The eyes are approximately halfway between the top of the head and the chin, and about an eye's width apart. The head is about five eyes' wide at eye level.

- Eyebrows are at the same level as the tops of the ears, while the bottom of the nose is usually level with the bottoms of the earlobes.
- The bottom of the nose is halfway between the eyes and the chin. The edges of the nostrils line up with the inner corners of the eyes. The corners of the mouth line up with the pupils.
- The centre of the mouth is one-third of the way between the bottom of the nose and the chin.
- The neck extends straight down from the bottom of the ears. This line curves slightly inwardly towards the shoulders – more in women and less

in men. The width of the shoulders is equal to two head lengths for a male; less for a female.

All faces are different, of course, but all fall roughly into these sorts of dimensions. The most popular portrait angles are full face (straight-on), profile and three-quarter views.

Because of the effects of foreshortening, the above proportions apply only if you have the same eye level as your sitter. If you are viewing the person from above or below, these proportions become distorted.